Quantum Leap
Preparing Blockchain Systems for the Era of Quantum Computing

Table of Contents

Chapter 1. Introduction

In this Special Report, we delve into the intersection of two revolutionary technologies: blockchain and quantum computing. This isn't just a dry technical breakdown. Instead, we journey into a future where these pioneering technologies come together, shaping a world enriched by unprecedented security and computational power. The report, "Quantum Leap: Preparing Blockchain Systems for the Era of Quantum Computing," eases you into the complex world of blockchain and quantum mechanics, elucidating the potential vulnerabilities of existing systems and proffering strategic solutions. Filled with real-world examples, future forecasts, expert insights, and actionable strategies, this report is a must-have for anyone interested in future-proofing their blockchain systems against the advent of quantum computing. Explore beyond the buzzwords and step confidently into the future with this comprehensive guide.

Chapter 2. The Convergence of Technologies: An Overview of Blockchain and Quantum Computing

Since their conception, blockchain technology and quantum computing have each stood as singular innovations with the capability to disrupt industries and change the world. While blockchain brings transparency and universality to digital transactions, quantum computing shatters the limitations of computation as we know it. It is here, at the intersection of these two transformative technologies, we stand to witness a new dawn of digital reality.

2.1. The Genesis of Blockchain

Blockchain emerged in 2008 when a person or group under the pseudonym Satoshi Nakamoto published a whitepaper for Bitcoin, the world's first decentralized digital currency. The brilliance of bitcoin was not in the currency itself, but in the technology that underpinned it: the blockchain. This public ledger design ensures that every transaction is transparent, verifiable, and immutable.

In essence, a blockchain is a chain of blocks. Each block contains a list of transactions, and once a transaction becomes part of the blockchain, it is practically impossible to alter. How is this done? Miners solve complex mathematical problems to form a block, and when a new block is formed, it joins the existing chain, creating an irrevocable link to the preceding block via a cryptographic hash. This distributed, decentralised system of trust has seen applications beyond cryptocurrency and is now being utilized in healthcare, supply chain, banking, and more.

2.2. Rise of Quantum Computing

Quantum computing was first proposed by physicist Richard Feynman in 1982. While traditional computers use bits, quantum computers use quantum bits (qubits), which exploit the unique properties of quantum mechanics. A qubit, relying on the phenomena of superposition and entanglement, can exist in multiple states at once, hence can handle an enormously larger set of data than binary bits.

Quantum computers can solve complex problems at exponential speed, which no traditional computer can manage within a reasonable timeframe. Encryption cracking, drug discovery, weather prediction — the potential applications of quantum technology are vast and can transform every sector.

2.3. Confluence of Blockchain and Quantum Computing

As blockchain continues to revolutionize data security and transactional integrity across industries, the rise of quantum computing threatens to destabilize it. Quantum computers, due to their superior computation capabilities, can potentially break the cryptographic algorithms that protect blockchains.

For blockchain systems, security depends on the difficulty of cryptanalysis — decrypting information without knowing the encryption key. Currently, it's thought that even the most powerful classical computers would take centuries to crack the cryptographic guards of blockchain. Yet, once we have scalable quantum computers, that could change dramatically.

Quantum threats aren't limited to blockchain. Every industry that uses cryptography for security, including all banking and information technology systems, is at risk. To safeguard the benefits and potential of blockchain technology, it's crucial to quantum-proof it sooner rather than later.

2.4. Quantum Resistance: Adapting for the Future

The race is on for cryptography resilient to quantum attack — quantum-resistant algorithms (QRAs). The National Institute of Standards and Technology (NIST) is leading a global initiative to standardize QRAs, and a handful of blockchain pioneers are integrating these into their systems.

Yet, for established blockchains, transitioning to QRAs will undoubtedly be disruptive and come with a significant cost. In response, experts propose a two-pronged defense: not just developing QRAs, but also quantum key distribution (QKD). QKD uses quantum entanglement to create pairs of keys such that any observation of the key changes its state, alerting the communicating parties to an intrusion.

Applying such solutions into existing blockchain systems could provide an extra layer of security resilience in the quantum era, offering not just defense against quantum computing, but also harnessing its strengths. Investment in research, open dialogue, and planning is necessary to ensure we're prepared for the day when quantum computing becomes the norm.

To conclude, the collision of the blockchain and quantum computing worlds presents a paradox — an extraordinary opportunity coupled with an existent threat. While blockchain brings potential for transforming systems of trust on a global scale, quantum computing poses a profound risk to its security. At the same time, quantum computing offers unrivaled computational power and new opportunities for industries across the board. This intricate meshing and clashing promises to create an exciting, unprecedented chapter in the annals of technological evolution.

Our responsibility in navigating this juncture is clear: continue exploring and investing in these technologies, while also preparing for their convergence. It's not too late to begin this journey; in fact, we are perfectly poised in the present to build future-proof systems, capable of leveraging the strengths of both blockchain and quantum computing, while ensuring robust security in the quantum age.

Chapter 3. Understanding Quantum Computing: From Basics to Blockchain Applications

Quantum computing is based on principles derived from quantum mechanics, the branch of physics that describes the quirky behavior of very small particles. At a basic level, a quantum computer maintains a sequence of qubits – equivalent to the 'bits' in a conventional computer – which can assume a much wider array of values than the binary 1s and 0s due to a property called superposition. Further, a pair of qubits can also exist in a state known as entanglement, where the state of one directly influences the other.

3.1. Quantum Bits: Qubits

This subsection takes us into the heart of quantum computing: the qubit. These quantum bits are at the core of quantum computing. Compared to classical bits -1s and 0s- qubits can represent numerous possible combinations of 1 and 0 simultaneously. This is due to the aforementioned property: superposition.

Qubits can be both 0 and 1 concurrently, and this is not a 50/50 split. Instead, it's defined by direction. When measured, there's a certain probability that the qubit ends up being either 0 or 1. But until it's measured, that qubit represents every possible combination of 0 and 1.

3.2. Quantum Entanglement and Superposition

Quantum entanglement allows for pairs of qubits to be linked in such a way that the state of one qubit can instantly influence the state of the other, no matter the distance between them. This fundamental piece of quantum computing allows for a level of complexity and interconnectedness that is impossible in classical computing models.

Superposition, on the other hand, allows for both a 0 and a 1 to exist simultaneously in a quantum state. Imagine a coin spinning in the air; it is not just heads or tails, but both at once. When it falls and lands, it adopts one specific state, just as a superposition collapses upon measurement to reflect a 0 or a 1. The concept of superposition makes a qubit exponentially more powerful than a traditional binary bit.

3.3. Quantum Gates and Circuits

Quantum gates act as operations or manipulations applied to qubits. Intriguingly, in the quantum realm, these operations can be executed on superposition states, not just the static 1s or 0s we see in classical computing. Furthermore, these gates are reversible, meaning that they can execute undos without losing information.

Similarly, a quantum circuit is a series of quantum gates arranged to perform a specific quantum computation. The gates in a quantum circuit interact with the qubits to produce an output, an operation that could be compared to—but is vastly more complex than—the functions of a classic electrical circuit.

3.4. The Potential of Quantum Computing

Quantum computers can solve certain tasks significantly faster than classical computers can. This is due to their ability to simultaneously assess every possible solution to a problem, leveraging the concept of superposition. Additionally, quantum computing promises improved capacity for machine learning, more accurate modeling of natural systems, and profound impacts on cryptography.

3.5. Quantum Computing and Blockchain

Blockchain technology is reliant on cryptography, which could be disrupted by the rise of quantum computing. As of today, blockchain uses classical digital signatures, but these are not resistant to quantum attack. A powerful enough quantum computer could theoretically perform a 'brute force' attack to find a private key given the public key.

Therefore, once quantum computers become commonplace and powerful enough—although this is a future that may still be some years away—it is inevitable that they will revolutionize blockchain technology. Future-proofing these networks for quantum resilience is thus critical.

3.6. Preparing for Quantum Blockchain

The advent of quantum computing necessitates that we rethink and repurpose our security protocols. Post-quantum cryptography (PQC) is a discipline dedicated to researching cryptographic algorithms that are secure against quantum attack. Transitioning to PQC will require diligent planning and execution, but it is a necessary step towards ensuring the security of blockchain technologies in the quantum future.

In conclusion, understanding quantum computing is the cornerstone of preparing blockchain systems for the era of quantum computing. Just as blockchain technology can offer radical shifts in how we transact and trust, so too can quantum technology bring about seismic changes. The intersection of these two revolutionary technologies is where the future of secure, efficient, and robust distributed systems lies. The key to unlocking it rests in understanding the quantum world, and this chapter represents the first step in that thrilling journey.

Chapter 4. Blockchain Uncovered: A Deep Dive into its Quantum Vulnerabilities

For decades, public key cryptosystems such as RSA and Elliptic Curve Cryptography (ECC) have served as the backbone for the security and privacy of the internet. At the core of blockchain technology lies this same principle of public key cryptography. However, the emergence of quantum computing threatens to shake the very foundation of these cryptographic systems.

4.1. The Deficiencies of Classical Cryptography

The security of cryptosystems like RSA and ECC is derived from the mathematical difficulty of certain computational problems, namely factoring large numbers and solving the discrete logarithm problem. Both of these processes remain secure under the guidelines of classical computing, as there is no efficient algorithm to solve them quickly. This security paradigm is decentralized, transparent, and highly secure, which has bolstered blockchain's utility in a myriad of use cases, like financial transactions and contract executions.

However, our confidence in these public key cryptosystems is rooted in the limitations of classical computers. Bounded by the 'bit' – a binary unit that can either be a '0' or a '1' – classical computers can only process particular states sequentially. Consequently, the overwhelming magnitude of possibilities when factors or logarithms grow large makes factoring and the discrete logarithm problem time-consuming and computationally expensive. Because facing an ordinary computer with such challenges is akin to locating a specific grain of sand on an endless beach, as the size of the numbers used in the algorithms increases, the security of these cryptosystems gets stronger.

It is crucial to understand, however, that this security doesn't stem from the cryptographic algorithms themselves. Instead, it relies upon the lack of computational power in classical computers. This reliance is where the advent of quantum computing strikes at the heart of this crypto-based security infrastructure.

4.2. Quantum Computing: A New Frontier

Quantum computing represents a fundamental shift from the classical computing model. Instead of bits, a quantum computer uses quantum bits, or 'qubits.' Because they exploit the principle of superposition in quantum mechanics, qubits can exist in multiple states simultaneously, rather than just '0' or '1.' And where traditional bits process data linearly - one piece at a time - qubits interconnect through quantum entanglement, allowing them to process multiple pieces of information simultaneously.

What are the implications of this for cryptography?

4.3. Quantum Computing and Cryptography

Shor's algorithm, formulated by Peter Shor in 1994, unleashes the full potential of these quantum features. It demonstrates that a quantum computer can factor large numbers and solve the discrete logarithm problem efficiently. Therefore, it directly challenges public key cryptographic systems backing blockchain technology. This vulnerability raises a significant concern regarding the security and integrity of the blockchain systems currently in operation. If a quantum computer of enough stability and power were to unexpectedly spring into existence today, virtually all traditional cryptographic systems, including blockchain, would be left defenseless.

4.4. Quantum Threat to Blockchain

Blockchain technology, as it stands today, is not quantum-resistant. For instance, Bitcoin adopts the Elliptic Curve Digital Signature Algorithm (ECDSA) for its key generation protocol. With the rise of quantum computers and Shor's algorithm, an adversary could derive the private key from the public key - a feat deemed impossible with classical computing. This vulnerability provides an opportunity for malicious actors to forge blockchain transactions and contravene the decentralized, tamper-resistant nature of blockchain systems.

Admittedly, quantum computers of such power are not yet upon us. However, the advance of quantum computing is brisker than commonly presumed, with some experts suggesting we could witness a quantum computer capable of breaking RSA and ECC in the next 10 to 20 years. Given the substantial lead time needed to upgrade and secure networks, the question is not if we prepare but when and how.

4.5. Embracing Quantum-Resistant Cryptography

The potential vulnerabilities presented by quantum computing demand proactive preparation. Quantum-resistant cryptography represents a hopeful avenue. These cryptographic methods, also known as post-quantum cryptography, are designed to secure against both classical and quantum computers. Initially, transitioning blockchain systems to new hash functions and digital signature standards would bolster their resilience against a quantum attack.

Promising quantum-resistant algorithms include Lattice-based cryptography, Hash-based cryptography, Code-based cryptography, and Multivariate polynomial cryptography. These frameworks resist current quantum algorithms and offer potential solutions to future-proof blockchain technology.

Integrating quantum-resistant cryptography with blockchain systems is a monumental task, demanding substantial resources, manpower, and expertise. It's also a critical process given the severe consequences of blockchain cryptographic systems failing. Therefore, the time to recognize quantum as a credible threat and initiate the migration process towards more quantum-resistant security measures is now.

In conclusion, despite the formidable strength and promise of quantum computing technology, it must not be understood as a death sentence for blockchain. On the contrary, it presents a chance to bolster the undergirding cryptographic infrastructure and further solidify the security of decentralized systems. But this necessary advancement insists upon immediate recognition and strategic action to preempt the quantum threat and foster a quantum-resistant blockchain landscape.

Chapter 5. The Quantum Threat: Potential Impacts on Current Blockchain Systems

Before venturing into the interaction of quantum computing and today's blockchain systems, it is essential to understand these technologies individually.

Blockchain can be defined as a decentralized and distributed ledger. It enhances overall transparency and erases the need for a governing body or middleman to ensure the legitimacy of transactions. Its primary strength lies in its cryptographic algorithms, which defend against data alteration and fraud thereby anchoring the foundation of contemporary cryptocurrencies.

On the other hand, quantum computing is a propitious innovation that deploys principles from quantum physics to process information exponentially faster than classical computing. Quantum systems operate on qubits (quantum bits) that unlike classical bits - which are either a 0 or a 1, use the superposition property to be in multiple states simultaneously. This empowers quantum computers to solve complex tasks at a marvelous pace, including breaking down today's most sophisticated cryptographic algorithms.

5.1. The Quantum Era vs. Current Cryptographic Systems

Bitcoin, the flagship of blockchain systems, is secured through a cryptographic method known as the Elliptic Curve Digital Signature Algorithm (ECDSA). This algorithm ensures secured financial transactions, authenticated identity, and legal non-repudiation. However, the ECDSA, like other cryptographic systems, is largely sustained by the complexities intrinsic in factorizing large integers - a task infeasible for classical computers but tractable for quantum machines, opening an avenue for potential threats in terms of security breaches and cyber attacks.

In alignment with Moore's law, classical computing capacity has been consistently rising, prompting cryptographers to occasionally increase keys' length to counteract the threat. However, the advent of quantum computing throws this effort off balance. Since quantum computers solve problems exponentially faster, they could crack the ECDSA and similar encryption methods significantly sooner than anticipated.

Similarly, hash functions, another cornerstone of blockchain systems, could also be prone to quantum attacks. These features protect previous transactions and make blockchain systems resilient against tampering but, intricate quantum algorithms like Grover's could crumble this layer of security by finding the input of a hash function given its output. This "quantum speedup" would accelerate the brute-force search, destabilizing the security balance in blockchain systems.

5.2. Quantum Computing: The Double-Edge Sword

Here's the paradox: while quantum computing jeopardizes today's blockchain systems, the blockchain itself might be a supportive tool to build a scalable quantum computer.

A quantum computer requires quantum bits to be "entangled" meaning the state of one qubit can instantly affect the state of another, no matter the distance. However, maintaining this entanglement in large-scale systems presents a formidable challenge due to "quantum decoherence," stemming from interference from the external environment. Quantum error correction codes are required to make quantum computers feasible and scalable, which are theoretically possible but pose significant practical problems.

In this context, blockchain technology could offer a solution by providing a decentralized ledger for highly transparent and secure record keeping of quantum states. This blockchain-powered method could mitigate quantum decoherence and lead to more scalable quantum computers.

Meanwhile, quantum-based cryptocurrencies are being developed as well, aiming to provide a degree of quantum resistance against attacks. However, their efficiency and security still remain subjects of extensive research and optimization, with a long pathway to commercial viability.

5.3. Preparing for a Quantum Future

While the arrival of universal quantum computers might be a couple of decades away, it is crucial to develop quantum-resistant blockchain systems today. Quantum-resistant cryptographic algorithms, notably Lattice-based, Hash-based, Code-based, and Multivariate Polynomial cryptography, present promising solutions to the quantum threat. There is urgency to shift efforts towards the deployment of these alternative cryptographic methods to safeguard blockchain systems.

Moreover, the post-quantum cryptographic transition should be smooth and timely, necessitating immediate research and revamping of blockchain systems to support a quantum-resistant algorithmic arsenal, every step taken now is towards a secure future.

It is important to remember that the dance of quantum computing and blockchain is a concerned tango. In the light of exponential computational possibilities, the quantum threat to blockchain systems is real and imminent. Nonetheless, turning the tables, blockchain technologies might prove instrumental to the realization of large-scale quantum computers. Therefore, preparing for a quantum future involves both nurturing and taming this uncertain dance between quantum computing and blockchain systems.

Chapter 6. Preparing for Quantum Invasion: A Look at Quantum-Resistant Blockchain

With the rapid march of technology, the era of quantum computing swiftly approaches. Quantum computers represent an evolution in computing power that could potentially break established cryptographic systems, and as a result, pose a significant threat to blockchain technology. Faced with this imminent quantum invasion, it is crucial that we prepare our blockchain systems to be quantum-resistant. In this section, we will examine the perceived threats, highlight the efforts already underway to safeguard blockchain technology, and elucidate strategies to further strengthen these systems for the quantum era.

6.1. Quantum Threat to Blockchain

A core feature of blockchain technology is its security. Distributed across a network of computers, a blockchain is resistant to modification because altering any single block requires consensus from the network. However, this level of security assumes that an attacker doesn't hold more than 50% of the computational power of the network. This is where quantum computers come into play.

Quantum computers operate on radically different principles than classical computers. Instead of binary bits that are either 0 or 1, quantum computers use quantum bits or 'qubits', which can simultaneously be 0 and 1. As a result, they promise exponential leaps in processing power that could potentially surpass the entire computational capacity of classical networks, breaking the 50% barrier.

The predominant security danger from quantum computers comes from their speculated proficiency with Shor's Algorithm. Designed to factor large prime numbers, this algorithm, if successfully run on a quantum computer, could shatter the encryption techniques used to secure information on the blockchain.

Primarily, blockchain uses digital signatures based on the mathematical problem of integer factorization. In simpler terms, it is currently infeasible for classical computers to derive the original two prime numbers from their product, making the system highly secure. However, quantum computers using Shor's Algorithm could also solve such problems more efficiently than classical computers, undermining the cryptographic functions that protect blockchain systems.

6.2. Quantum-Resistant Blockchain Efforts

Parallel to the steady advancement of quantum computing, efforts are being launched to develop quantum-proof cryptographic protocols. Post-quantum cryptography is a subfield devoted to the development of cryptographic systems that are secure even in the presence of a quantum computer.

One prevalent example of a new cryptographic algorithm proposed as a solution is the Lattice-Based Cryptography. This technique revolves around problems in a high-dimensional lattice structure that are currently not known to have quantum algorithms for their solution. So, even though they might be simpler for a classical computer to solve, they are equally difficult for both quantum and classical machines.

Another technique being proposed is Hash-Based Cryptography. This methodology takes advantage of the fact that quantum computers don't significantly speed up hash functions, which are a one-way function to convert data into a set format.

It's essential to remember that both these techniques, while promising, also come with their trade-offs. Lattice-Based Cryptography can be cumbersome and affect system efficiency, while Hash-Based systems may demand more memory or involve shorter key lifetimes.

6.3. Strategic Actions for Quantum-Resistance

Transitioning to a quantum-resistant blockchain is not a trivial task. However, by identifying potential risks and developing strategic actions, it is possible to mitigate the possibility of quantum-based threats. Here are several key strategies:

- **Early adoption:** Given that replacing cryptographic systems can be a prolonged and complex process, it can be beneficial to adopt post-quantum cryptography algorithms earlier rather than later.

- **Hybrid systems:** Implementing a combination of classical and quantum-resistant algorithms can provide an additional layer of security while maintaining interoperability with existing systems.

- **Open research and collaboration:** Collaboration among scientists, researchers, and industry professionals will speed up the development and standardization of quantum-resistant cryptographic systems.

- **Periodic key replacement:** Implementing a system where keys are frequently replaced can make a blockchain more resistant to quantum decryption attempts, even when using techniques like Shor's Algorithm.

In closing, the advancement of quantum computing undeniably challenges the present security measure employed in blockchain technologies. However, these challenges also stimulate innovation in the sector, driving the creation of more robust and future-ready systems. Understanding these potential threats and preparing for them will allow us to continue leveraging the benefits that blockchain offers as we step into a future reshaped by quantum computing.

Chapter 7. Real-World Cases: Quantum Computing in Blockchain Today

In line with the current technological revolution, it is becoming evident that true pioneers are those who dare to conceptualize the seemingly impossible, hence the foray into the union of blockchain and quantum computing. Let's explore some compelling real-world applications wherein these two technologies have intersected.

7.1. Quantum Resistant Ledger (QRL)

Quantum Resistant Ledger (QRL) is an example of a project started to recognize and address the possible risks associated with quantum computing pertaining to blockchain. QRL combines the effective aspects of blockchain, such as immutability and transparency, with the potential processing power that quantum computing can provide.

One of the major worries concerning blockchain technology is the aspect of security. Blockchain relies heavily on cryptographic processes, particularly those that would currently be unbreakable by classical computers. However, quantum computers pose a substantial risk due to their immense computing power. QRL aims to mitigate this risk by utilizing post-quantum cryptographic methods to secure the blockchain.

QRL leverages the Extended Merkle Signature Scheme (XMSS), a post-quantum security protocol, guaranteeing strong security assurances due to its utilized hash-based cryptography. The hash-based cryptography is known to resist quantum computing attacks, which inherently increases the security level of blockchain interactions on the QRL platform.

7.2. Quantum Blockchain – The Russian Quantum Center

The Russian Quantum Center have taken a novel approach to the convergence of quantum computing and blockchain. They have developed a quantum blockchain that is theoretically tamper-proof, leveraging quantum mechanics' uncertainty principle. This uncertainty principle, at its most basic, means that you cannot accurately or simultaneously know pairs of physical properties of a particle, such as position and momentum.

Their Quantum Blockchain uses quantum entanglement as part of the blockchain validation process. Each block added to the chain entangles with every previous block, making the entire blockchain quantum entangled. If an attacker were to try and change a transaction in a previous block, it would break the entanglement and simultaneously destroy the information in the other blocks that and thus alerting the network.

This revolutionary approach opens up a realm of possibilities in enhancing blockchain security in ways that we couldn't have envisioned before.

7.3. qBittorrent

The 21st century is the age of information, and with the immense expansion of the Internet, information sharing has never been more important. Torrent systems have been at the forefront of file sharing, but they too are not without their share of vulnerabilities.

qBittorrent, despite having a similar name to the popular torrent client, is intended to be a fully decentralized, anonymous, and quantum-resistant torrenting system. It employs QRL's post-quantum secure blockchain and the InterPlanetary File System (IPFS) to create a protocol that combines the advantages of blockchain and quantum computing to decentralize file sharing and resist cybersecurity threats. Furthermore, IPFS identifies files by their content, ensuring the correct file is always delivered to the user, thereby reducing the risk of receiving corrupted or tampered files.

7.4. Post-Quantum Cryptography Standardization (NIST)

With the advent of quantum computing and its potential risks to currently utilized encryption standards, the National Institute of Standards and Technology (NIST) initiated the Post-Quantum Cryptography Standardization process. Although this is not a distinct entity like QRL, Russian Quantum Center, or qBittorrent, it is a critical consideration for blockchain developers and other cryptography-reliant technologies.

One of the critical tasks undertaken by NIST is the identification and standardization of quantum-resistant cryptographic algorithms, which will eventually replace the ones currently under quantum risk. Furthermore, NIST's public competition model encourages the international cryptographic community to contribute, enhancing the solution's robustness and applicability.

In conclusion, the merging of blockchain and quantum computing isn't merely theoretical but is gradually manifesting in diverse applications worldwide. These real-world cases mark the beginning of ensuring that the blockchain systems are prepped for the era of quantum computing. The path includes, but is not confined to, post-quantum cryptographic systems, quantum blockchains, quantum-resistant torrenting systems, and international standardization initiatives. While we journey into a future shaped by these technologies, we must emphasize research and development to harness their potential fully.

Chapter 8. Pivotal Players: Leading Figures and Companies in Quantum Blockchain

The future is quantum, and there's no denying the crucial role certain personalities and organizations are playing in propelling these technologies to the forefront. As our society becomes more intertwined with digital systems, the need for secure, trustworthy, and powerful solutions become imperative. This is where the pivotal players in the arena of quantum blockchain come into play.

8.1. Fascinating Figures

As we peruse this realm, the first person to note would be Artur Ekert. A professor at Oxford University, Ekert is one of the founders of quantum cryptography. Back in the 90s, Ekert introduced the concept of entanglement-based quantum key distribution, a mechanism to generate secure random keys utilizing quantum properties. His work drove further research in quantum cryptography, ultimately fostering the integration of quantum computing with blockchain technology to enhance network security.

Shor Peter, an MIT professor, deserves mention here as well. Shor is the mathematician behind Shor's algorithm, a quantum algorithm that could factorize large numbers exponentially faster than the best-known algorithms running on classical computers. His contributions sound a warning for today's blockchain systems which rely heavily on classical cryptography, raising the critical need for developing quantum-resistant algorithms to guard against such a threat.

Among these influential figures is also Michele Mosca, a professor at the University of Waterloo and co-founder of the Perimeter Institute for Theoretical Physics. Known for his profound work in quantum algorithms and complexity, Mosca predicted that there's a 1-in-7 chance that quantum computing could break RSA-2048, a commonly used cryptographic scheme, by 2026. His forecast adds to the urgency of preparing our blockchain systems for the quantum era.

Let's not forget Seth Lloyd, an MIT Professor, who developed the first quantum algorithms for fast Fourier transform and period finding. His research signifies the potential of quantum computers to solve complex problems faster than classical counterparts, offering an outlook into the impact quantum computing could have on blockchain's computational capabilities.

8.2. Companies Advancing Quantum Blockchain

Turning our gaze now to the companies that are carving paths in quantum blockchain, we begin with QC Ware. Based in the heart of Silicon Valley, QC Ware is exploring the merger of quantum computing with blockchain. With its robust quantum software, the company aims to accelerate the application of quantum computing in industries like finance, where blockchain is a key player.

Another firm worth noting is QuantumX, a Canadian start-up that is designing and developing quantum-secure blockchain solutions. They aim to provide a commercial, off-the-shelf quantum-safe security solution to meet the quantum threat.

Then we have Qiskit, an open-source quantum computing software development framework led by IBM. Qiskit provides the tools needed to create quantum computing programs and run them on quantum computers. The framework's cryptography library, which includes quantum versions of classical cryptographic schemes, is a notable contribution towards making blockchain systems quantum-resistant.

The Chinese technology giant, Alibaba, has also entered the scene through Alibaba Cloud. They offer advanced quantum solutions and have published several research papers pertaining to quantum cryptography. This includes a recent one on quantum digital signatures – a security mechanism pivotal to blockchain technology.

Another worthy addition to this list is Quantropi, which uniquely leverages quantum mechanics to deliver perfect secrecy over the public internet. Their solution, QEEP™, is designed to be quantum-safe and promises to provide the highest level of data protection in our evolving digital world.

Lastly, let's talk about Qilimanjaro Quantum Tech. Based in Spain, this quantum services company envisions building a consortium of users, developers, and researchers to expand the reach and potential of quantum technologies. They foresee a decentralized quantum computing service, facilitated by a blockchain-based ecosystem. A system that, when achieved, promises greater computing power and data security in the age of quantum computing.

In conclusion, these stalwarts and their respective organizations are playing vital roles in preparing present blockchain systems for the impending quantum era, a future both exciting and daunting. Through their continuing efforts, the development of a quantum-secure world appears less a question of 'if' and more a matter of 'when'.

Chapter 9. The Looming Quantum Reform: Regulation and Policy Challenges

Blockchain technology has ushered in an era of decentralized trust, breaking traditional centralized ways of transacting, recording, and verifying information. On the other hand, quantum computing, with its immense computational power, promises to revolutionize data processing and encryption methods. These two technologies are intersecting, and this intersection is neither simple nor effortless. The challenges, although substantial, extend beyond mere technical adjustments. With this union, we're paving the way for entirely new regulatory landscapes, leading us into the realm of quantum reform.

9.1. Quantum Computing: An Overview

Before delving into quantum reforms and their impact on policies and regulations, let's grasp what quantum computing is. In essence, a quantum computer takes advantage of the quantum phenomena - superposition, entanglement, and interference - to process information. Unlike classical computers that transact in bits (0s or 1s), quantum computers use quantum bits, or qubits, allowing them to potentially solve problems beyond the reach of classical machines.

9.2. The Looming Challenge: Quantum Threat to Blockchain

Blockchain's security is fundamentally based on cryptographic principles. The robustness of blockchain comes from complex mathematics that make cracking the codes computationally intensive. However, with quantum computing, these strong cryptographic standards are under threat. The prime concern is that quantum computers could potentially reverse-engineer public private-key pairs. If attained, this could enable illicit access to all transactions in a blockchain, shaking the very foundations of the trust such systems usually engender.

9.3. Exploring the Regulatory Landscape

Blockchain's decentralization, coupled with quantum computing's disruption, encompass a host of regulatory challenges that policymakers need to adequately address for the technologies to fuse successfully.

- Privacy Implications: Quantum computing poses a significant threat to data privacy. Regulating data access, securing it from illicit intrusion, and governing how companies handle quantum-encrypted data will be paramount.

- Standardization: As early as now, it is crucial to establish widely accepted standards for quantum-safe cryptography that blockchain developers can implement.

- Intellectual Property: Questions concerning the ownership and control of quantum technologies will inevitably grow as the technology matures. Policymakers must work towards transparency, fair use, and non-discriminatory practices in this area.

9.4. Crafting Quantum-Resilient Regulations

To safeguard the decentralized architecture of blockchain from quantum threats and to foster trust, proactive regulatory measures must be set in place. Adopting quantum-safe cryptographic methods is a clear path forward. Technologies such as lattice-based cryptography, error-correcting codes, code-based cryptography, multivariate cryptography, and their ilk appear promising.

However, we must acknowledge that just as regulations need to be adaptable for technology, the technology must likewise adapt to regulatory needs. A long-term perspective that emphasizes resilience, flexibility, and preparedness is hence important. This will better stave off sudden shocks should quantum computing advance faster than expected.

9.5. Global Cooperation and Policy Harmonization

Given the global nature of these technologies, attempting to confine their reach within national boundaries is unwise. The ideal way forward is through global cooperation and policy harmonization.

This fosters an environment conducive for the effective and secure application of blockchain and quantum technologies. A global treaty addressing quantum threats to private key infrastructure across all nations could offer a solid starting point. Stakeholder collaboration - involving governments, tech companies, academia, and other influencers - will be key to surmounting these challenges.

The journey from understanding the quantum threat to drafting quantum-resilient policies and regulations will not be easy - it will require proactive coproduction of knowledge, dialogue, and continuous revisits to existing standards. The world needs to come together in crafting a resilient response to this inevitable quantum reform.

In this new era, the power of blockchain systems lies not just in the underlying technology but also in their interplay with policies and regulations. The "Quantum Leap" requires not just a technical shift, but also substantial regulatory and policy changes. The reform is looming, and we need to engage in thoughtful deliberations on these challenges to prepare for it sufficiently. The potential of blockchain, if combined effectively with quantum-safe measures, promises a future unprecedented in its security and computational possibilities. But we are only as robust as our weakest link. The future awaits us, and it is up to us to take the initiative.

Chapter 10. Future Projections: Quantum Computing and Blockchain in 10 Years

It is crucial to note that predicting the exact future of any technology, and more so for revolutionary technologies like blockchain and quantum computing, is an elusive challenge at best. However, based on current progress and deductive reasoning, this chapter sets forth what might be expected in the realm of quantum computing and blockchain within the next ten years.

10.1. Quantum Computing: A Decade Down the Road

In a decade, quantum computers, no longer relegated to mere concept or advanced research labs, will likely have made significant strides towards everyday applicability. According to forecasts from IBM and other researchers, quantum computers compliant with fault tolerance—the ability to correct quantum errors—should be operational by the end of the decade. This would allow quantum computers to perform incredible amounts of calculations simultaneously, thereby solving complex problems faster than ever thought possible.

Just as classical computers experienced tremendous advances over their first few decades, quantum computers in ten years will likely be characterized by increased hardware stability, superior scalability, better qubits quality, and improved error correction mechanisms. Coming years will also see a rich ecosystem of quantum software, quantum algorithms, and substantial improvements in quantum communication and security protocols.

10.2. Blockchain: Vision for 10 Years

In parallel to the advancements in quantum computing, blockchain technology in ten years will have progressively evolved—moving beyond transactions and cryptocurrencies to permeate diverse applications like supply chain traceability, digital identity management, voting systems, and more. Blooming alongside quantum technology, blockchain should be well-equipped to survive and thrive in the budding era of quantum computing.

The blockchain of the future will not only be about decentralization but also about scaling and interoperability. Solutions for problems like scalability, speed, and transaction costs should be well-established, leading to the widespread adoption of the technology across different sectors. New consensus algorithms are likely to emerge, improving on the energy efficiency and making blockchain sustainable.

Blockchain technologies will become essential components of Web 3.0, with decentralized applications being as common as smartphone apps are today. Blockchain will be as inconspicuous yet fundamental as HTTP is for the internet, underpinning secure, transparent and frictionless interactions in an increasingly digital world.

10.3. Quantum-Blockchain Intersection: Future Perspectives

The crossroads of quantum computing and blockchain offer a compelling glimpse of what the future might hold. Without doubt, the superior computational power of quantum computers could pose a threat to the encryption that secures blockchain. However, the more pressing concern is that the advent of quantum computing could render current cryptographic mechanisms obsolete, hence exposing blockchain applications to new vulnerabilities.

Some experts predict that by leveraging the capabilities of quantum computers, it would be possible to break through a blockchain's cryptographic security. However, this so-called quantum threat would take at least a decade to materialize, if not more. This ten-year window provides ample time for blockchain technologies to adapt, thereby transitioning to quantum-resistant cryptographic mechanisms.

Additionally, quantum computers could supercharge blockchain processing, eliminating scalability issues that plague certain current systems. Quantum blockchains, an area under intensive research, could achieve unparalleled security, tamper-evidence, and transparency levels, presenting a whole new paradigm for decentralized systems.

10.4. Quantum-Resistant Gates: Bolstering Blockchain Security

While it might seem like quantum computers and blockchain are headed for a collision course, the future is not all doom and gloom. Throughout history, as threats to cryptographic systems have emerged, so too have solutions to counteract them. This trend is expected to continue with the evolution of quantum-resistant cryptographic algorithms, which are constructed in a way that makes them immune to the computational superiority of quantum computers.

There's a growing body of research in post-quantum cryptography that focuses on developing mechanisms to secure digital communications against a potential quantum computing breach. This will likely lead to a new generation of blockchain systems that are robust against quantum attacks, a critical step for the enduring relevance of blockchain technology. Quantum-resistant blockchains, designed to withstand the computational power of quantum computers, will not just become commonplace but mandatory.

10.5. Decentralized Nature: A Unique Strength

A key advantage of blockchain is its inherent decentralization. Quantum computers, with their profound processing power, will undoubtedly be challenging to build, expensive to maintain, and complex to operate. However, the decentralized nature of blockchain means that even if a quantum computer could break a single link in the chain, it wouldn't compromise the entire network. This built-in resiliency could make blockchain technology all the more valuable in a quantum future.

10.6. Emerging Quantum Blockchains

The field of quantum blockchains is a nascent one but has the potential to redefine how security is viewed in the quantum age. Quantum blockchains elevate the security of distributed systems to a whole new level, leveraging quantum cryptography and quantum entanglement to ensure that any attempt at data manipulation can be swiftly identified and rectified.

10.7. Conclusion and Future Directions

The co-evolution of quantum computing and blockchain brings together two revolutionary technologies that have the power to redefine our digital landscape. Within the next decade, as the quantum era unravels and blockchain continues to mature, unforeseen applications of their convergence will emerge.

Continued research and optimization of both technologies will be crucial in preparing the digital world for their full integration. With blockchain's evolution in step with quantum computing advancements, organizations should stay informed and prepare for quantum-readiness.

Indeed, the nexus between blockchain and quantum computing is creating an entirely new discipline in computing science. Just as blockchain has fuelled the rise of a decentralized economy, quantum computing promises to fuel unimaginably complex problem solving and data processing. In tandem, they pave the path for a world that marries the assurance of security with unprecedented computational power.

Chapter 11. Actionable Strategies: Safeguarding your Blockchain Systems against Quantum Attacks

As we navigate the future of blockchain and quantum computing, the word of the day is undoubtedly preparation. By understanding the potential threats posed by quantum computing and structuring our blockchain systems accordingly, we can ensure that our operations are not only poised for progress, but protected against any potential quantum threats. This chapter aims to furnish you with a suite of strategic solutions that could be employed to secure your blockchain systems from the anticipated rise of quantum computing.

11.1. The Quantum Threat to Current Blockchain Systems

Quantum computers, flourishing in their potential to process mathematical problems at unprecedented speeds, elicit benefits and challenges in equal measure. One significant area of concern pertains to encryption algorithms, which are a cornerstone of blockchain systems. Blockchain, by its distinctive design, hinges on cryptographic security for maintaining its chain of blocks. Alas, the encryption that current blockchain systems employ could be vulnerable to quantum attacks.

Shor's algorithm, devised by mathematician Peter Shor, permits quantum computers to factor large numbers exponentially faster than classical computers. This algorithm directly threatens RSA and Elliptic-curve cryptography (ECC), which support most of today's blockchain systems. Put simply: the security mechanisms currently employed by blockchain systems could crumble beneath the power of quantum computing.

11.2. Quantum-Resistant Blockchain: A Necessity, Not a Luxury

Given these threats, it's clear that we cannot remain inert. Blockchain systems must evolve to combat the emergent quantum threat. This leads us to the concept of quantum-resistant blockchains.

In essence, quantum-resistant blockchains employ non-factor based cryptography. Unlike RSA and ECC, they aren't vulnerable to the factorizing capabilities of Shor's algorithm. By incorporating quantum-resistant cryptographic algorithms into blockchain systems, we can render them resistant to quantum attacks. However, to effectively integrate these algorithms, it's important to understand the variants available in the quantum-resistant cryptographic landscape and their respective advantages and constraints.

Several quantum-resistant algorithms have come to the fore over the past decade, including Hash-based, Code-based, Lattice-based, Multivariate polynomial, and Supersingular elliptic curve isogeny cryptography.

Hash-based cryptography is one of the most mature quantum-resistant alternatives available and is regarded as being particularly robust. Code-based cryptography is another secure option, though it demands more memory and fails to offer forward secrecy. Lattice-based algorithms are promising for their versatility and potential for other applications like fully homomorphic encryption.

The path to the future isn't clear-cut. Rather than stating one cryptographic method as superior, it's incumbent upon us to assess the suitability of methods for distinct systems and requirements. This takes us to our next focus: integrating quantum-resistant cryptography into blockchain systems.

11.3. Integrating Quantum-Resistant Cryptography into Blockchain Systems

While alluding to the need for transition to quantum-resistance in blockchain systems, caution is necessary. Shifts of such magnitude require due diligence, extensive testing, and step-by-step implementation.

Initially, the design and architecture of the blockchain system must be revisited. Introducing a new cryptographic method isn't a standalone task, but touches every part of the system, from block generation and validation to consensus mechanisms.

Ensuring backward compatibility is also crucial. Existing users shouldn't be left behind in the shift towards quantum-resistance. To do so, a dual system approach could be effective. This entails maintaining the old cryptographic method while simultaneously offering the new quantum-resistant method. Consequently, users can switch to the new system at their own pace.

Versioning of different cryptographic methods can help manage these transitions. This allows for introducing or retiring cryptographic methods according to their relevance and security. An agile process of versioning ensures the lifespan and adaptability of the blockchain system, making it continuously resistant to emerging threats.

Lastly, a significant factor of this integration, which is often underestimated, is user education. Users should be made aware of why the transition to a quantum-resistant blockchain is necessary, its implications, and how can they make the switch smoothly.

11.4. Regular Audits and Blockchain Hardening

Regular audits of the blockchain system are crucial to maintaining its robustness against quantum threats. As a safety net, they reveal vulnerabilities and provide opportunities for improvements.

The objective of an audit is to examine the blockchain across three principal areas: cybersecurity aspects, cryptographic methods, and regulatory compliance. External auditors with expertise in quantum-resistant cryptography and blockchain technology are best equipped to provide a comprehensive audit and recommend modifications.

Blockchain hardening, similar to system hardening in computer security, refers to performing all possible actions required to secure a blockchain network. This involves regular patching, maintain user privilege levels, and employing multi-factor authentication.

11.5. Quantum Threat Intelligence

In the ever-evolving cryptographic landscape, it's vital to keep abreast of trending threats and vulnerabilities. Staying informed helps anticipate threats and develop countermeasures proactively.

To attain quantum threat intelligence, a combination of in-house research, external threat feeds, and community involvement can be utilized. Collaborating with academia, industry think tanks, and participating in cybersecurity forums can offer insights deeper than silo-based research activities.

This chapter aimed to outline various strategies to safeguard your blockchain systems against quantum threats. However, it's essential to remember that the landscape of these pioneering technologies is dynamic. Therefore, continuous learning, adaptability, and agility remain key to staying ahead of the curve. As we embrace this brave new world of quantum computing and blockchain, preparedness is our most potent weapon.

www.ingramcontent.com/pod-product-compliance
Lightning Source LLC
Chambersburg PA
CBHW061055050326
40690CB00012B/2633